Sex
The Way To Do It Right According To The Brain.

David Gomadza

www.twofuture.world

Copyright © 2024 David Gomadza

All rights reserved.

PAPERBACK ISBN: 9798324502904

DEDICATION

A better world.

CONTENTS

ACKNOWLEDGMENTS

Tomorrow's World Order

SEX. THE WAY TO DO IT RIGHT ACCORDING TO THE BRAIN

Sex
How the body deals with sex
Sex is something that every person on earth must experience one way
or the other sex is there as a reset switch itself sex makes us who we are
there is no organism that cannot experience over time for reproduction
to occur there must be some sex going on now if we are to ask a lot of
questions these are the questions
What was
What can be
What would be
What was but that can't be
What can be but how
What is but not now
What would be but when
What can be
What would be and what could be
Now if we Ask anyone what they think about sex then this is the
answer sex is sucaremnorolt meaning godly and forever wonderful that
means everything on earth look forward to having sex at some point
this is the way life is now if we are to ask some critical questions here
they are sex is there was there and will always be there forever if sex can
be changed and swapped with something else the answer is that sex can
and in fact is swapped with self-help activities like personal gratification
through masturbation but if we Ask what could be of sex this is the
answer we get sex could be better Intimacy can be increased and
performance be upgraded what could be of sex sex can be elevated to a

new level where there are other things to argument it if we are to ask
these are the questions
Can sex be increased in scope
Can sex be elevated to another level
Can sex be intricate meaning housed so that it magnifies individuals
Can sex be enhanced to new ways
Can sex be highlighted as a hobby or sports activity people can enjoy
regularly there are taboos regarding sex promiscuous sex can lead to
death if we are to ask what can be what is the answer
Sex can be enjoyable and fulfilling but how do humans do the actual
activity these are all brain commands related to sex and in specific order
1 askforsex.start
2 ifrejecteddontstopstartagain.start
3 ifacceptedthenstart.sex.now
4 whatif.start
5 whatcanbe.start
6 whatcouldbe.start
7 whatwasandwhatcouldbe.start
8 oncestarteddontstop.start
9 onceinsidedontstop.start
10 onceheisinsidestartdontstop.start
11 ifnotcumdontstopbutspeedup.start
12 whatcanbeofsex.start
13 whatcouldbeofsexdontstopcontinue.start
14 onceinsideejsculate.start
15 onceheisinsidelethimejaculate.start
16 ifnotcumhelp.start
17 ifnotcumwhileindidehelp.start
18 onceoutsidesexisboringbutwecanstartagain.start
19 oncehecumsexidboringbutdontstopforyourturnstart.dtart
20 ifarousedagain.start
21 ifnotarousedagainmakewayforsexagain.start
22 wheninsidesgaindontstopbutcontinuefast.start
23 whenheisinsidestart.start
24 onceinsidedontstopkeepmovinglick.start
25 ifnotinsidemakehimputin.start
26 startdontstopaskformoresexboth.start
27 whensatisfiedsleep.start
28 whenstillhungrybeg.start.start
29 ifnotenoughdontbeshyaskagsinanndagainuntilhappy.start
30 ifhappysayiloveyou.start

31 ifnothappysayplease.start

32 askdontstop.start

33 sayhisex.start

34 nowlickbreastsfirst.start

35 lickballs start

36 lickchest.start

37 lickvagina.start

38 licknaval.start

39 lickhumberg[pussyhumb]sayoh.start

40 askhername.start

41 askhimpenisname.start

42 askifshecansucktoo.start

43 askifhecanlickbetweentitstoo.start

44 askifhecancumonnaval.start

45 askifshecansquirtinhisface.start

46 askifshecanwankinhisface.start

47 askifshecansuckinhisface.start

48 whatif.start

49 whatifyouhadmalesexorgsnshowwouldyoulikesucked.start

50 askifhehadfemaleorganshowwouldhelikedtobelicked.start

51 whatcanbeofsex.start

52 whatcouldbeofsex.start

53 whstwasofsex.start

54 whatisofsex.start

55 whatmightbeofsex.start

56 whatwasofsex.start

57 whatifofsex.start

58 whatcouldbeofsex.start

59 whatifofsex.start

60 whatwouldbeofsex.start

61 ifnotthenwhat.start

62 whatcanbeofsex.start

63 whatcanbeofsex.start

64 whatisofsex.start

65 whatisofsex.start

66 whatisofsex.start

67 ifnotnowthenwhat.start

68 whatissex.start

69 whatissex.start

70 ifnotmethenwho.start

71 whatcanbeofsex.start

72 whatissex.start

73 ifnotnowthenwhen.start

74 ifnotcome.start

75 whatistobe.start

76 canwestart.start

77 whatcanbeofsexwithyou.start

78 sexstartwithmenow.start

79 whatisofsex.start

80 sexifnotsexthenwhat.start

81 whatissex.start

82 canwefuck.start

83 ifsexwhencum.start

84 howfast.start

85 whatif.start

86 whatcanbeofsexandus.start

87 whatissex.start

88 whatcanbeofsex.start

89 sexwithyou.start

90 lickmyneck.start

91 lickmychest.start

92 lickmyvagina.start

93 lickmynipples.start

94 lickmyclit.start

95 smarkmyclithard.starr

96 lickmyvaginaandspitonitandrubit.start

97 spitonmytitsandrubthemhardandsqueeze.start

98 nowsaybitchfingeringmyvagina.start

99 askifican [but stop]

100 sayyouwanttofucknowbitch.start

101 sayfuckmenow.start

102 sayiwantitnowcome.start

103 ifnotnowthenwhen.start

104 askforpenetrationsexily.start

105 onceinsayisthatall?.start

106 asksoftlyifhecum.start

107 askifhecancumnow.start

108 saywhytakelongwheniamfast.start

109 saycumnowinmypussy.start

110 saywhenyoucum.start

111 askwhen.start

112 askwhatif.start

113 askwhatcanbe.start

114 askwhatthefuck.start

115 askwhatwasofsex.start

116 askwhatcanbeofsex.start

117 askehenofsex.start

118 askwhatwasofsex.start

119 whatcanbeofsex.start

120 whatisofsex.start

121 whstcanbeofsex.start

122 whatisofsex.start

123 whatwasofsex.start

124 whatisofsex.start

125 ifnotnowthenwhen.start

126 whatcanbeofsex.start

127 whatwasofsex.start

128 whatissex.start

129 whatissex.start

130 whatwouldbeofsex.start

131 whatwasofsex.start

132 wwhatissex.start

133 whatissex.start

134 whatcanbe.sex

135 sex.start

136 sex.start.now

137 whatwasofsex.start

138 whatcanbeofsex.start

139 whatifofsex.start

140 whatcanbeofsex.start

141 whatwasofsex.start

142 whatisofsex.start

143 sex.start.now.continue.start

144 sexifnotnowwhen.start

145 sexletsstart.start

146 ifwefuckletsdoitnow.start

147 whatcanbedoneofsex.start

148 ifnotsexthenwhat.start

149 sex.start.now.now.start

150 ifnotsexthenwhat.start

151 whatcanbeofsex.start

152 sexcanbesexbut.start

153 sexissexwithyou.start

154 sexissex.start
155 whatissex.start
156 sex.sex.sex.start
157 whatcanbesaidofsex.start
158 whatissex.start
159 ifnotus.start
160 sexcanbesex.start
161 sexissexbut.start
162 ifsexthenwhat.start
163 sexassexbut.start
164 canwedonow.start
165 whatcanbeofsexwithyou.start
166 sex.sex.sex.start
167 ifnotusandnotnowthenwhat.start
168 whatisromp.start
169 removeyourknickers.start
170 ilickyourchest.start
171 Icanaskagainandagainsexwithyou.start
172 istillwantcome.start
173 ifnotisthenwho.start
174 letsstartsexagain.start
175 iamwet.start
176 iamhornyforyou.start
177 letsfuckallnight.start
178 letsdonow[demanding-clithard].start
179 whstwasofsexandwhatisnow.start
180 whatcanbeofsex.start
181 whatissex.start
182 ifnotsexthenwhst.start
183 sex.start
184 ifnotsexthenwhat.start
185 whatissex.start
186 whatifwearetothenwhat.start
187 ifnotnowthenwhat.start
188 whatcouldbe.start
189 ifnotsexthenwhat.start
190 ehatwouldbeof.starr
191 whatcanbeofsex.start
192 ifnotsexthenwhat.start
193 whatissextoyou.start
194 ifpossible.start

195 whatifofsexyouandme.start
196 tobelovedintgeend.start
197 sayiloveyou.start
198 sayiknow.start
199 ifwecan.start
200 sex.stop.sleep
Now we have looked at all brain commands regarding sex but what if
we need to expand our vocabulary how would we go about this? The
brain over time learn how to talk sex it forms language it understands
but one related to sex overtime it tends to use shorthand language that
depicts sex but might not be sexual in nature now let's look at how the
brain does this the brain will form lines it will associate with sex these
lines will act as memory lanes whenever it wants to think about that sex
thoughts the lines are illuminated so that when a thought is reached the
lines become dime as the thought is extracted back to the brain then
the lines are temporarily removed until after the thought is sent back if
we are to ask what can be done this is the answer we can create cells
instead of lines that can be used for sex memory so that instead of rail
lines that fades and become prominent the cells can simply send the
memory straight to the brain as needed without the fading now if we
are to ask what can be of sex then this is the future sex can be made
safe and secure and more enjoyable by use of toys and gadgets that aide
sex if we are to ask what could be of sex then sex could be anything but
if we are to substitute sex then this is how we would do it
Sex for a hobby
Sex for self help
Sex for dancing
Sex for asking
Sex for not asking [reverse programming]
Sex for music
Sex for eating [binge eating]
Sex for sewing
Sex for art
Sex for yoga
Sex for climaxing with toys
Sex is like a cliffhanger in that if not satisfied will remain unresolved
just like a cliffhanger must be resolved and this is how to resolve sex
cliffhangers
Ask the person who caused the arousal for sex that removes that
cliffhanger offer to buy her a drink instead drinks replaces quests for
sex in that the cliffhanger is the same but the resolution is quite easy

drink and all is gone and now forever sex is a taboo for some people as it's something that can't be talked about but what if we can talk and think about sex can we openly admit that we are sexually attracted to others or its a taboo as well whatever the case sex can be intimidating to ask for but then again everyone have their reasons for or for not asking for sex.

If we Ask the brain what it thinks about sex and what are the benefits this is the answer sex is an addiction for all as it must be done on a daily basis for men and regularly for women sex is a cliffhanger that must be satisfied in the end sex is a herb that heals without the organic compound sex satisfies soothes and comforts most if not all find solace in sex those who don't might have alternatives to sex like killing others that brings same gratification now if we look at sex as a body function here are the commands for sex first for a woman

Initiates.start
Oncestartedsexcantbestopped.start
Ifhornyfingervaginafirst.start
Ifhornylicknipplesecond.start
Ifhornyaskfordick.start
Ifhornylookatdicks.start
Ifhornylickyourlowerlip.start
Ifhornystartvaginacornermassage.start
Ifhornywhynotaskforakiss.start
Ifhornyrubnipplesthoroughly.start
Ifhornywetyourknickersabdlookatit.start
Ifhornylookinyourknickers.start
Ifhornyaskhowcome.start
Ifhornyaskforsexnicely.start
Ifhornyfingervagina[,middle].start
Ifhornystartarousal.start
Ifhornylicklipsoften.start
Ifhornyaskforsex.start
Ifhornyaskwhynot.start
Ifhornyaskwhatif.start
Ifhornyrubvaginalipshardtoburn.start
Ifhornywhisperaguysname.start
Ifhornyaskwhynotnow.start
Ifhornyaskwhatcanbedone.start
Ifhornyaskwhatcanbedone.start
Ifhornyashwhatifbut [then stop]
Ifhornyrubnipplesonebyoneuntildrooling.start

Ifhornyrubnipplesjustrightside.start
Ifhornyaskaguytosuckbreast.start
Ifhornyaskaguytosuckrightnippleonly.start
Ifhornyasktolicktitsofman.start
Ifhornyasktoseepenishood.start
Ifhornyasktoseepenisshaft.start
Ifhornyasktoseetesticles.start
Ifhornystartvaginalmassage.start
Ifhornystartfullvaginalmassage.start
Ifhornyaskforablowjob.start
Ifhornyaskforahandjob.start
Ifhornyshowmanvagina.start
Ifhornyshowmanbreasts.start
Ifhornyshowmaninsidevagina.start
Ifhornyshowmanknickersandcrotch.start
Ifhornysecretlyfingervaginainpublic.start
Ifhornysecretlysqueezebreasts.start
Ifhornystart.start
Once all done in order then do next lot of activities preferably in that order for intense orgasms that lifts everything up to highest level in a woman all this according to the brain Now you must also do the following activities
Asktowatchamanwankhardbutwithoutejaculationstophiminthemiddle.start
Asktoseeamanrubballshard.start
Askamanogglehervagina.start
Askamanoggleherbreasts.start
Askamanogglehernipples.start
Askamanogglehervaginalips.start
Askamanoggleherhumberg.start
Askamanslapherclithard.start
Askamanslapherbuttockshard.start
Askamantearapaperinherface.start
Askamandroolinherface.start
Askamaninticeherlegstoopen.start
Askamantopushopenherlegs.start
Askamanslaphergroin.start
Askamansaybut[then stop].start
Askamansaybutwhatif.start
Askamansaywhatthefuck.start
Now after that you must do the following for an intense experience

Askamantosuckhardrightnippleonly.start
Askamansuckhardallnipples.start
Askamanslapherclithard.start
Askamanslaphergroingard.start
Askamanslapeverythingonherhard[breasts vagina nipples clit ass].start
Now wait before next step possible 2 minutes now Ask the man to
Fingervagina.start
Fingerass.start
Fingermouth.start
Fingervaginathenass.start
Squeezetitshard.start
Squeezebuttocks.start
Rubclit.start
Rubvaginahard.start
Rubrimhard.start
Rubnippleshard.start
Rubass.start
Rublabiamajore.start
Rublabiaminore.start
Rubtits.start
Cuptits.start
Cupass.start
Salivateandspitonvagina.start
Salivateandspitonnipplesandaskmantosuck.start
Salivateandkissaman.start
Soilknickerswithprecum.start
Askforvaginamassagebut[refuse first holding his hand].start
Nowacceptvaginalmassageandspreadhard.start
Askwhatifhehadavaginahowwouldhewantitmassaged.start
Askifhehadbrwastshowwouldhewantedthemcupped.start
Now open wide and invite the man in the rest it's action and depends
on you and him by now the body is ready all spots are highlighted and
ignited all ready to explode.
Now we look at what to do if you are a man
Askwhatcanbedone.start
Askwhatistobe.start
Askwhathasbeen.start
Askwhatcouldbe.start
Askwhatcanbe.start
Askwhathasbeen.start
Askwhatwas.start

Askwhatthefuck.start
Now look at a woman with awee and ask for sex
Askwhatifshehadadick.start
Howwouldsheliketobesucked.start
Askifshehadballshowwouldsheliketobelicked.start
Now look at her in the eyes and deep enter and reach for the soul point right back side of the head ask if we can be soul mates. Wait for reply and follow reply.
Now once soulmate sex is out of this world arousal is not just mutual but intensified
Now
Askwhatifbut[then stop].start
Askwhatcouldbe.start
Askwhatcanbedone.start
Askwhatcouldbebut[then stop].start
Nowaskwhatwasbutcouldbe.start
Askwhatwasbut.start
Whatcanbedone.start
Whatistobe.start
Whatwas.start
Whatcanbe.start
Whatwouldbe.start
Whatistobe.start
Whatistobe.start
Whatwas.start
Whatistobe.start
Whatcanbe.start
Whathasbeen.start
Whatisandisnotofsex.start
Now
Ask her what can be done
Now
askwhatcanbeofsex.start
Now she should be ready just as you just a couple minutes away from orgasm but remember sex is about mutual respect and trust.
The End

THE FUTURE OF SEX

Sex will forever remain sex but can be aided by toys and Wearable Brain Books.

Visit www.twofuture.world

ABOUT DAVID GOMADZA

Visit www.twofuture.world

Sex. The Way To Do It According To The Brain.

15

16

www.ingramcontent.com/pod-product-compliance
Lightning Source LLC
Chambersburg PA
CBHW031358250726
48656CB00012B/2371